THE I Love You More BOOK

Written by Debby Herbenick, PhD

Illustrated by Rosalie Orlando Hatch

StoryPeople Press

ISBN-13: 9781937137991
ISBN-10: 1937137996

StoryPeople Press
P.O. Box 7
Decorah, IA 52101
USA
563.382.8060
563.382.0263 FAX
800.476.7178

storypeople@storypeople.com
www.storypeople.com
www.storypeoplepress.com

Library of Congress Control Number:2011934321

First Edition: October, 2011

THE I Love You More BOOK

Written by Debby Herbenick, PhD
Illustrated by Rosalie Orlando Hatch

For James, who I love more than all the stars
And Lucy, who I love bigger than Mars.
- D.H.

To James, R.O.H

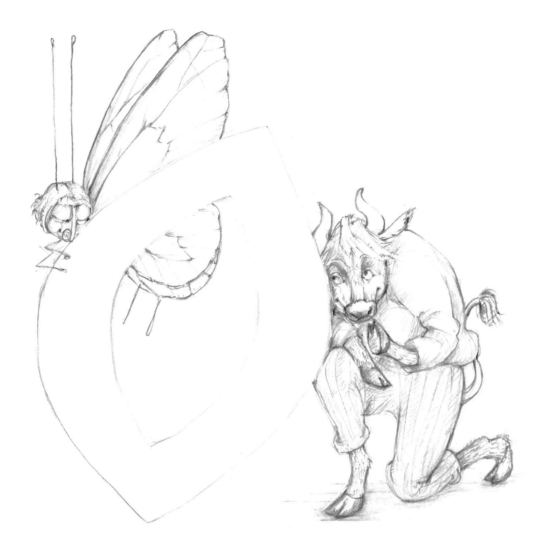

Once, on a day that was much like today,
A Bull and a Butterfly came out to play.
They'd been close together for many a year
And had names for each other like Honey, Darling and Dear.

On this day the butterfly said to her friend,
"How do I know that our love will not bend?"
The bull took one look at the love of his life,
Held a hoof to his heart and said, "Even a knife
On this spot wouldn't cause as much pain
As living without you through nine thousand rains.
My love is much bigger than all of the fuzz
On all of the sheep that ever there was,
On all of the farms since the beginning of time.
It's big, I tell you, so big and sublime."

The butterfly said she loved him more than infinity,
Then flew in a circle and said, "It's got to be
More than that, I know it,
But I can't seem to show it.
So tell me, big strong bull of mine,
Why, year after year, do you call me Valentine?"
"Because I love you more than all of the dimples
On every last golf ball, it's really that simple!

I'm sturdy and strong and my love's twice as big
As the snout on the world's most gargantuan pig.
Tall as the tallest giraffe on a mountain.
Full as the spray in the world's biggest fountain."

The butterfly fluttered her beauteous wings,
Alive with the joy that only love brings.
"Well, I love you more," she whispered, and smiled,
"Than all of the creatures who run in the wild.
The lions and tigers and quick gazelles, too.
All running and leaping, that's how I love you.

I love you so many, the number I said,
I'll multiply by all the things that are red.
Apples, tomatoes, balloons, roses, too.
Plus everything bright green or deep vivid blue.
Did you stop to think what a big number that becomes?"
The bull said, "Dear, I'm afraid it seems more than mine sums."

"But it can't be," he snorted, "since I love you more
Than every last door knob on every last door
Times the number of stars that you see in the night
Times the number of stars that you don't see but might
Wish to, you see, on a night such as this.
A night when lonely ones long for those that they miss.

And that's just a start to the infinite number
I dream of each night as I drift into slumber.
My deep admiration then soon multiplies
By the number of presidents, prisoners, and spies!

It's large, I can tell you, as large as the sun
Times the fish in the sea and the bands on the run
Times the number of bounces all balls ever made
Times the number of people who drink lemonade
While sitting on porches in summer or spring
Times the number of jewels of each queen and king."

The bull paused and looked at his butterfly dear
Who had flown to a branch to be ever more near.
She looked this way and that with her thinking cap on,
And she spoke with a passion that shone like the dawn.
"My goodness, if that's not a tough one to beat.
Though I'm sure with my heart, I am able to compete."
So she flew up and down, then landed on her friend's nose.
She hummed a little tune and said that her love grows
And blooms more times than all of the flowers
On all of the planets in fall and springtime showers.

"Those flowers," she said, "you can't see when they grow.
But, with our love, you don't need to look to know
How big and tall and abundant is our love.
I say, Big Strong Bull, when push comes to shove,
I'll love you longer than quarter past silly.
Longer than the blades of grass on earth, flat or hilly,
Taped together in one super-long, spiraled string
Times the number of off-key songs that I can sing.

Our cares are one hundred times higher
Than any airplane or rocket ship flier.

When I wake in the morning to hear such bull snores,
That are often ninety-seven times as loud as lion roars,
I feel happy knowing that you're my forever-best friend
And that inside-safe feeling tells me our love will not bend.
For if our love can outlast your deep snoring sounds,
Then larger and lovelier is our love by leaps and bounds."

The bull made a snort. The butterfly flew near.
He said, "Honey." She said, "Darling." He said, "Dear."
And that is the story of the twosome who know
They can touch feet, hands or hearts wherever they go.

About the Author

Debby Herbenick, PhD is a research scientist at Indiana University, a newspaper and magazine columnist, and author of *Because It Feels Good* and *Read My Lips*. Originally from Florida, she currently lives and loves in Bloomington, Indiana.

About the Artist

Rosalie Orlando Hatch was born in New York City and feels lucky to have lived near a beautiful park where she spent much time when growing up. Besides being a great place to play, it was later a great place to do landscape painting. She attended the High School of Art and Design and Queens College of the City University of New York.

Still in New York City and still close to a park, she lives with her family and spends time in the nearby woods where butterflies are easy to spot. Within walking distance is a farm, which while not home to a bull, does have cows, sheep, and pigs, all of whom were very helpful in making the pictures for this book.

About StoryPeople

StoryPeople Press is located in the heart of America (That's right... Iowa). Through its publications, StoryPeople Press strives to make the world a better place by spreading the words of laughter, imagination and inspiration. Visit www.storypeoplepress.com to see what other works are available.

StoryPeople features the work of Brian Andreas and includes StoryPeople sculptures, colorful story prints, and books, all available in galleries and stores throughout the US, Canada and the EU (along with a few others scattered about the world), and on their web site. Drop in on the web anytime at www.storypeople.com, or please feel free to call or write for more information:

StoryPeople Press
113 E. Water St.
Decorah, IA 52101
USA

866.564.4552
563.382.8932
563.382.0263 FAX

StoryPeople
P.O. Box 7
Decorah, IA 52101
USA

800.476.7178
563.382.8060
563.382.0263 FAX